# HELLO
This book belongs to:

To all teachers who inspire their students with creativity and fun!
-A.M.

Meet August
Text and Illustrations copyright ©2024 by April Martin
Calendar Kids Books, LLC | Kathleen, GA 31047
ISBN: (Paperback) 978-1-957161-21-1, (Hardcover) 978-1-957161-22-8
Library of Congress Control Number: 2024910271
All rights reserved.

No part of this publication may be used or reproduced in any manner, electronic or mechanical, including photocopying, recording, or any information storage or retrieval system, without prior written permission from the publisher.

To find out more about The Calendar Kids® Collection, visit www.calendarkids.com and sign up for newsletters or follow us on social media @thecalendarkids.

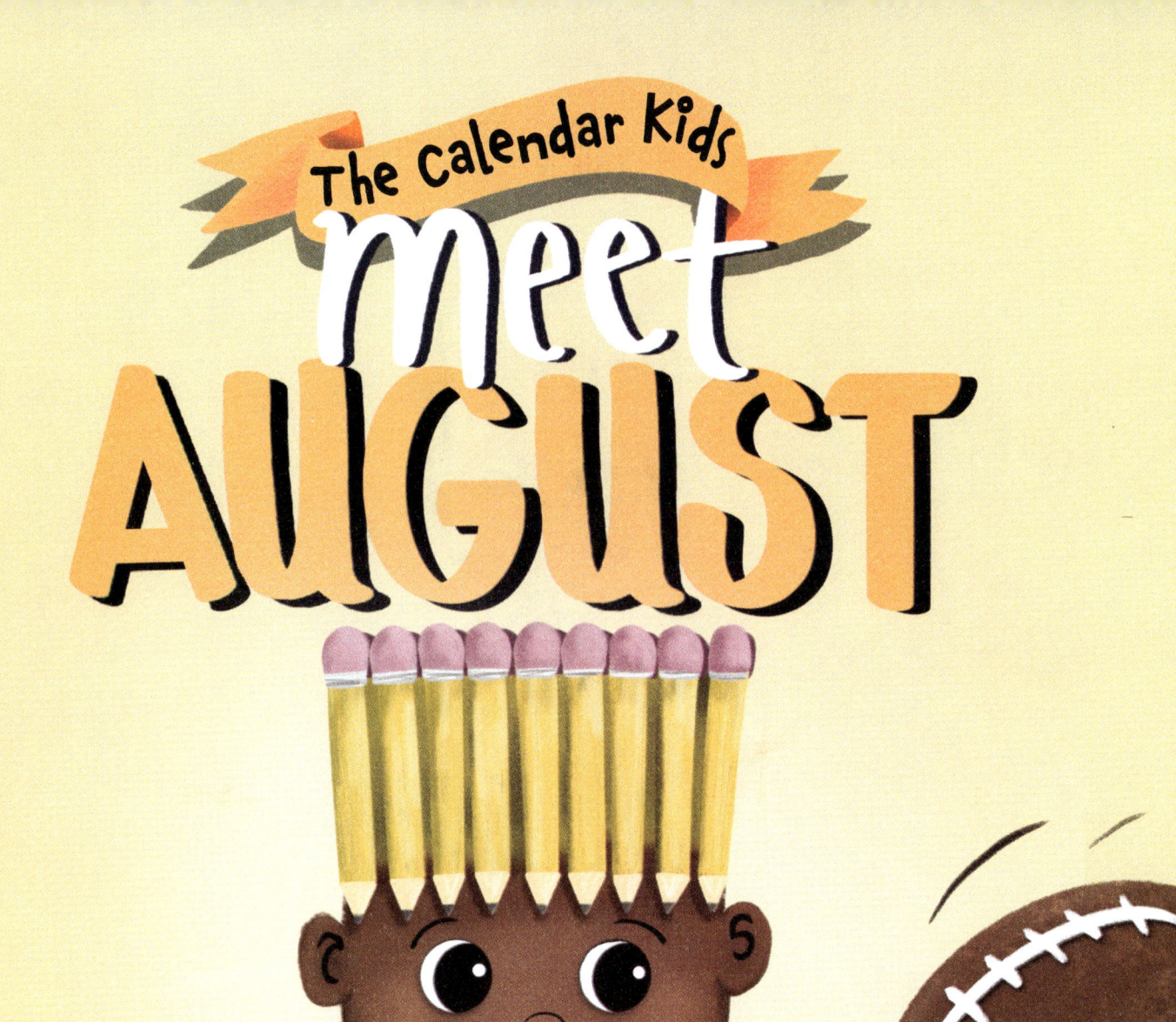

## The Calendar Kids
# Meet AUGUST

April Martin

This is August.

August loves the summer.
He loves a good chill day at home with no plans but to play.
He loves hearing the ice cream truck in his neighborhood too.
Eating a cold snack is a great way to cool off on a hot summer day!

August also loves football. He's excited to watch the preseason games on TV! Teams all over America are getting ready to play against each other.

One thing August doesn't love is getting sweaty. Sometimes when he plays football he gets soaking wet from sweat. Ew.

He misses throwing the football at school with his friends, but he knows school will start soon. He loves getting ready for the new school year too! He can't wait to see everyone again!

Every summer, August gets to pick out new school supplies. He picks out new markers and crayons to use. He loads up on paper and pencils. He loves the years when it's time for a new lunch box or backpack. This year, he gets to pick them out out for himself!

August also gets a fresh new haircut to start off the school year!

One year, he had long hair.

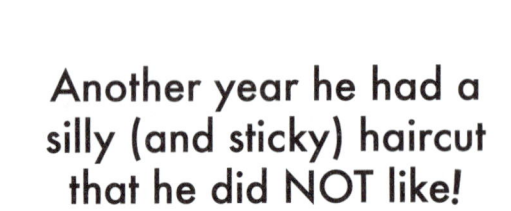

Another year he had a silly (and sticky) haircut that he did NOT like!

This year, he was excited to show off his new hairstyle.

The barber did a really good job! It was the perfect back-to-school haircut!

All summer break, August got to sleep in, watch way too much TV, and play with Sunny, his pet hamster. Each day, he marked off his calendar. Just one week left until school started back. His days off were coming to an end.

SUNDAY
MONDAY
TUESDAY
WEDNESDAY
THURSDAY
FRIDAY
SATURDAY
SWIM
1ST DAY!
CAMP
STOP
HAMSTER CARE SHEET

August loves to celebrate the end of summer with his closest friends, July and September. Before the new school year begins, they have one last play day in the sprinklers and set up a lemonade stand. It's their end-of-summer tradition!

Finally, the day had come... the first day of school! August was ready with his new pencils and paper, his new backpack and lunch box, and his cool new haircut too...

- ✓ pencils
- ✓ paper
- ✓ backpack
- ✓ lunch box
- ✓ COOL NEW HAIRCUT!

**First Day of School!**

... but for some reason, he still was nervous.

Would he see his friends in his class? Did he grow too tall this summer? What if his new teacher was mean?

The worst part of all, he had to walk to school, and the news reporter said it was going to be the hottest day of the year.

"What if I sweat too much and they all make fun of me?" August worried.

"Come on August, time to get going! We need to take the first-day-of-school picture!" His parents shouted from the front porch.

So August got up, got dressed in his new school clothes, brushed his cool new haircut in to place, and took a picture on the front doorsteps.

His mom made a fun back-to-school breakfast for him, complete with pencil-shaped waffles and a good luck message.

August finished his breakfast quickly. He did not want to be late on the first day back. He said bye to Sunny and started walking to school. "Oh no," he thought. "The news reporter was right. This has to be the hottest day in the history of ALL hot days. It has to be like... a hundred and ten degrees. I feel like I'm in an oven!"

August started to sweat...

... and sweat

and sweat

and sweat.

So he drank all of his water, but he could not stop sweating.

"Maybe I'm still a little nervous. Is it really hot enough to make me sweat this much?" August wondered.

By the time August got to school, he had sweat so much, he became a puddle!

ANNUAL ELEMENTARY

WELCOME BACK

He couldn't move. He just wiggle-wiggled, and he jiggle-jiggled...

He couldn't say hi to his new classmates.
He couldn't show everyone his cool new haircut.

"You can't be serious," January said.
"I've never sweat that much a day in my life."

August's closest friends, July and September, knew what to do.

"Oh, this happens ALL the time. He just gets a little too sweaty in the summer. Come on, August. Let's get you cooled off," July said to his friend.

July and September scooped up their friend and took him to the nurse. Ms. Ouchie helped August cool off. Finally, by the time school started, August was back to normal.

"Whew. That was not the way I wanted to start my day," he thought. But it was great having his friends walk in to school with him. He wasn't so nervous with them by his side.

July, August, and September walked down the hall to their new classroom. To their surprise, Ms. Seasons was their teacher this year. They love Ms. Seasons!

"Hello, friends. So nice to see you again," she said to the group.

Ms. Seasons's class was decorated for the new year. The students found their desks and hung up their backpacks. They even learned about their new schedule. First, they would go to the new music teacher, Ms. Melody, and then it was time for math and recess.

"Football!" August was thrilled. This was going to be a great school year!

The best thing August learned on the first day of school, was there was nothing to be worried about after all.

He saw lots of friends. He met new ones too!

He did grow too tall, but it wasn't a problem.

His teacher was definitely not mean.

And last but not least,
he learned to take the bus instead.

BLUE BUS

STOP

"Ahhh...
nice cold
AC."

# My August Notebook

Special August birthdays or events in my family:

The best part about the month of August is...

- August has 31 days.
- August is the eighth month of the year.
- The month after August is September.
- August is a summer month.
- If you are born in August, your birthstone is peridot.
- Did you know... Some schools start a new school year as early as July. Other schools start in September.
- Did you know... August is a hot month, but July is actually the hottest month in most places.
- National Friendship Day is the first Sunday in August. Do something fun with a friend!

# Discussion Questions

1. August loves seeing the ice cream truck. Name something you love to do in the summer.

2. August likes to watch preseason football games. What do you think the word "preseason" means?

3. August sweat so much, he turned into a puddle! Do you think that can really happen? Why do you sweat?

4. August was nervous about the first day of school. Were you nervous when you started school?

5. August got a new haircut. What do you think of it?

6. Did everything go OK on the first day of school even though it started off a little rough? Tell about a time your day turned around for the better.

7. Why do you think August chose to ride the bus instead?

# First Day of School Waffles

## You will need:

1 frozen waffle
1 chocolate chip
fruit of your choice
(strawberries, raspberries, or grapes)
toppings (optional): chocolate sauce, whipped cream, or maple syrup

## Directions:

1. Take your premade waffles out of the freezer and have a grown-up put them in the toaster and toast until light brown.
2. When they are ready, have a grown-up cut a rectangle and triangle shape out of the waffle like this.
3. Use your choice of fruit. Cut in half and place at the top of the rectangle; this will be the eraser.
4. Take one chocolate chip and place at the tip of the triangle. This will be your pencil point.
5. Write your name on your plate with chocolate sauce.
6. Top with syrup or whipped cream. Enjoy!

# meet APRIL

Author April Martin taught first grade for many years. She was always nervous on the first day of school, but she quickly got to know her new friends and everything went as planned. Now, as a mom, she enjoys making First Day of School Waffles for her own children.

**CALENDAR KIDS BOOKS**

To learn more about when the next Calendar Kids® books will be available, visit www.calendarkids.com!